EVERGLADES
NATIONAL PARK

BY KATHLEEN CONNORS

Gareth Stevens
PUBLISHING

Please visit our website, www.garethstevens.com. For a free color catalog of all our high-quality books, call toll free 1-800-542-2595 or fax 1-877-542-2596.

Library of Congress Cataloging-in-Publication Data

Connors, Kathleen.
Everglades National Park / by Kathleen Connors.
p. cm. — (Road trip: national parks)
Includes index.
ISBN 978-1-4824-1679-4 (pbk.)
ISBN 978-1-4824-1680-0 (6-pack)
ISBN 978-1-4824-1678-7 (library binding)
1. Everglades National Park (Fla.) — Juvenile literature. 2. National parks and reserves — Juvenile literature. I. Connors, Kathleen. II. Title.
F317.E9 C66 2015
917.59—d23

First Edition

Published in 2016 by
Gareth Stevens Publishing
111 East 14th Street, Suite 349
New York, NY 10003

Designer: Andrea Davison-Bartolotta
Editor: Kristen Rajczak

Photo credits: Cover, pp. 1 (right inset), 14 (bird) Brian Lasenby/Shutterstock.com; cover, p. 1 (left inset) Anthony Ricci/Shutterstock.com; cover, back cover, interior (background texture) Marilyn Volan/Shutterstock.com; pp. 4, 6, 8, 10, 12, 14, 16, 18, 20 (blue sign) Vitezslav Valka/Shutterstock.com; pp. 4, 6, 8, 10, 12, 14, 16, 18, 20, 21 (road) Renata Novackova/Shutterstock.com; pp. 4, 21 (map) Globe Turner/Shutterstock.com; p. 5 John A. Anderson/Shutterstock.com; p. 7 Walter Bibikow/Photolibrary/Getty Images; p. 8 Hoberman Collection/UIG via Getty Images; p. 9 (main) NASA.gov; p. 9 (inset) AridOcean/Shutterstock.com; p. 11 Tim Kiusalaas/Photographer's Choice/Getty Images; p. 12 Jupiter Images/Stockbyte/Thinkstock; p. 13 Diane Uhley/Shutterstock.com; p. 14 (panther) Steven Biandin/Shutterstock.com; pp. 14 (frog), 15 Rudy Umans/Shutterstock.com; p. 14 (manatee) Reinhard Dirscheri/Visuals Unlimited/Getty Images; p. 17 Steven Greaves/Lonely Planet Images/Getty Images; p. 18 Felix Lipov/Shutterstock.com; p. 19 (main) Leonard McCombe/Life Magazine/Time & Life Pictures/Getty Images; p. 19 (inset) Pedro Sostre/Wikimedia Commons; p. 20 Michael Lustbader/Photo Researchers/Getty Images; p. 21 (notebook) 89studio/Shutterstock.com.

Printed in the United States of America

CPSIA compliance information: Batch #CS16GS: For further information contact Gareth Stevens, New York, New York at 1-800-542-2595.

Contents

Words in the glossary appear in **bold** type the first time they are used in the text.

A Special Park

There's a park in the United States unlike any other place in the world! Everglades National Park is found at the southern tip of Florida, about an hour from the city of Miami. Its beauty, wildlife, and many plant **species** have drawn people's interest since long before it opened as a national park in 1947.

Everglades National Park **protects** about one-fifth of the Everglades. The Everglades are a **marsh** and grassy **region** covering more than 4,300 square miles (11,135 sq km) of southern Florida.

Tampa

St. Petersburg

ATLANTIC OCEAN

Florida

GULF OF MEXICO

Miami

■ **Everglades National Park**

Everglades National Park

where found: Florida

year established: parts became a state park in 1916; became a national park in 1934 (didn't open until 1947)

size: 1.5 million acres (607,500 ha)

number of visitors yearly: about 1 million

common wildlife: tree frogs, alligators, manatees, Florida panthers

common plant life: mangroves, orchids, white water lilies

major attractions: Shark Valley, Everglades Safari Park, Mahogany Hammock, HM69 Nike **Missile** Base

Everglades National Park is the third-largest national park in the lower 48 states.

Pit Stop

Post

Native Americans who lived around the Everglades called it "pa-hay-okee," which means "grassy water."

One and Only

Conservationist Marjory Stoneman Douglas said, "There are no other Everglades in the world. They are one of the **unique** regions of the earth. Nothing anywhere else is like them."

The Florida Everglades are the only place in the world called "everglades." That's not their only unique feature! The Everglades are the biggest **breeding** grounds in North America for wading birds. They're also the only place on Earth where alligators and crocodiles live together.

Pit Stop

A glade is a grassy area in a forest or swamp. Adding "ever" to the word could mean the seemingly never-ending nature of the glade in Florida.

Visitors to Everglades National Park can see the unique features of the Everglades.

Settlement and Misuse

People have been living in the Everglades region for about 15,000 years. Spanish explorers came in 1513, and settlers have lived near the park's present-day location since then.

During the 1800s, settlers started trying to drain water out of the Everglades in order to build and farm on the land. Birds and other wildlife were being overhunted for their feathers and hides. Conservationists began to worry about the **ecosystem** of the Everglades. In 1916, some land was set aside as Royal Palm State Park.

Pit Stop

Seminole Indians lived in the Everglades from the 1700s until the mid-1800s. The Miccosukee tribe still lives in the park with special government permission.

Florida

■ main image area

— greater Everglades ecosystem

— state protected lands and waters

Today, about half of the original Everglades have been destroyed. The main photograph shows how much city growth has occured in the area.

Establishing the Park

By 1934, the Everglades were nationally recognized as a special ecosystem in need of protection. That year, Congress approved Everglades National Park, though it wasn't established until 1947.

In the park today, visitors can learn about the special **habitats** that have been protected. These include the hardwood hammocks, which are stands of many kinds of trees, such as mahogany. Mangrove forests are found along rivers and streams. The word "mangroves" is used for many species of trees that can live in salt water.

Pit Stop

Mangrove forests are **nurseries** for fish. They also protect other parts of the nearby forests from strong winds and rain.

Many early national parks were created to protect natural beauty. Everglades National Park was the first one established to protect an ecosystem. Mangroves like these are one important part of this ecosystem.

Water Everywhere

Florida Bay is an estuary, or a place where salty seawater meets inland freshwater. This is one habitat visitors often enjoy—but it can be dangerous. The bay is covered in sea grass, and boaters have to be very careful of the shallow water the grass covers. Florida Bay is less than 3 feet (91 cm) deep on average!

One way water moves around the Everglades is the freshwater sloughs (SLOOZ), which are marshy rivers. Shark River Slough and Taylor Slough are found in the park.

Pit Stop

Visitors can see the wilderness of the Everglades up close by going slough slogging. A park ranger leads this off-trail hike a few times a week.

Shark River Slough is often called the "River of Grass," a fitting name as this photograph shows.

Animal Party

A major draw for visitors in Everglades National Park is the wildlife. Hundreds of kinds of animals live in the park, including about 400 bird species and 20 snake species. In addition, the Everglades have a high population of West Indian animal species, another feature making it a unique ecosystem.

Tree frogs, manatees, otters, and Florida panthers are some of the animals visitors can spot when visiting the park. Shark Valley, the Anhinga Trail, and Eco Pond are good places to watch for alligators, crocodiles, and birds.

Florida panther

Cuban tree frog

manatee

purple gallinule

Would you like to see an alligator? If so, Everglades National Park is a good place to go!

Pit Stop

Thirty-nine species of orchids can be found in Everglades National Park.

Protect

Everglades National Park might be the only place visitors can see some kinds of plants and animals. There are 113 plant species growing in the park that Florida lists as **endangered**. More than 20 endangered or uncommon animal species, including the snail kite, manatee, and alligator, are protected in Everglades National Park, too.

Conservation efforts in the park focus on restoring parts of the Everglades that have been harmed by people's activities. Some of this includes **monitoring** the populations of endangered species.

Pit Stop

Post

You can learn all about conservation at Everglades National Park! Talk to any rangers you meet, and visit one of the visitor centers to discover more.

Water covers about one-third of Everglades National Park! It's important to monitor the amount of water and its quality to keep all the habitats safe.

Natural Fun

There's a lot to do at Everglades National Park! At Everglades Safari Park, you can take an airboat ride around the park and see an alligator show. Canoes, boats, and kayaks can travel down all or part of the Wilderness Waterway Trail. It's 99 miles (159 km) long!

Biking, hiking, and camping are big parts of many visits to Everglades National Park. Viewing wildlife, such as birding, is a draw for many, too—just don't feed any animals!

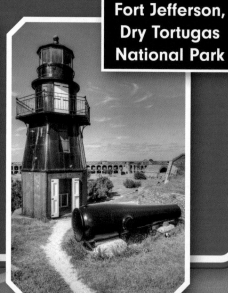

Fort Jefferson, Dry Tortugas National Park

Pit Stop

Post

To the north of Everglades National Park is Big Cypress National Preserve. To the east is Biscayne National Park, and Dry Tortugas National Park is to the southwest.

You can take a walk to the HM69 Nike Missile Base found in Everglades National Park. It's been inactive since 1979.

birdwatcher at sunrise in
Everglades National Park

Wet and Dry

The best time to visit Everglades National Park is between December and April. That's the dry season. The temperature only reaches about 77°F (25°C). The water levels in the park go down then. This causes the animals to seek out watering holes, making them easier to spot!

From May to November, the average high temperature is about 90°F (32°C)! It rains most days. Make sure to plan your trip to Everglades National Park with this in mind!

Pit Stop

There are 40 to 65 inches (102 to 165 cm) of rainfall in the Everglades each year. Most of that happens during the wet season.

Visiting
Everglades National Park

Miccosukee Indian Village

Everglades Safari Park

•Miami

Shark River Slough

Florida Bay

HM69 Nike Missile Base

Glossary

breeding: mating and giving birth

conservationist: a person concerned with conservation, or the care of nature

ecosystem: all the living things in an area

endangered: in danger of dying out

habitat: the natural place where an animal or plant lives

marsh: an area of soft, wet land

missile: a rocket used to strike something at a distance

monitor: to watch carefully

nursery: a place where young animals can grow and are cared for

protect: to keep safe

region: a large area of land that has features that make it different from nearby areas of land

species: a group of plants or animals that are all the same kind

unique: one of a kind

For More Information

Books

Furstinger, Nancy. *The Everglades: The Largest Marsh in the United States.* New York, NY: AV2 by Weigl, 2014.

Heos, Bridget. *Do You Really Want to Visit a Wetland?* Mankato, MN: Amicus, 2015.

Websites

DEP Kids Page—Florida Everglades
www.dep.state.fl.us/secretary/kids/postcards/everglades.htm
The Everglades need help. Learn more here!

Learning About the Everglades
www.nps.gov/ever/forkids/learning-about-the-everglades.htm
Visit the National Park Service page about the Everglades.

Index